The Number Crew Resource Book

Written by Marjorie Gorman
Illustrated by Juliet Breese
Designed by Town, London
Editors: Liz Meenan and Alec Edgington

ISBN: 1862155372

© 1999 Channel Four Learning

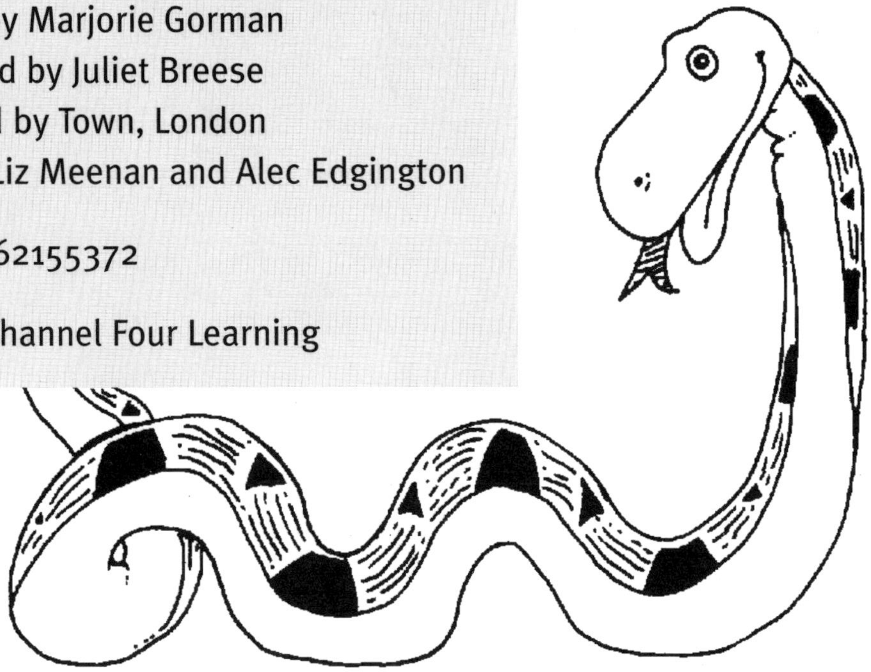

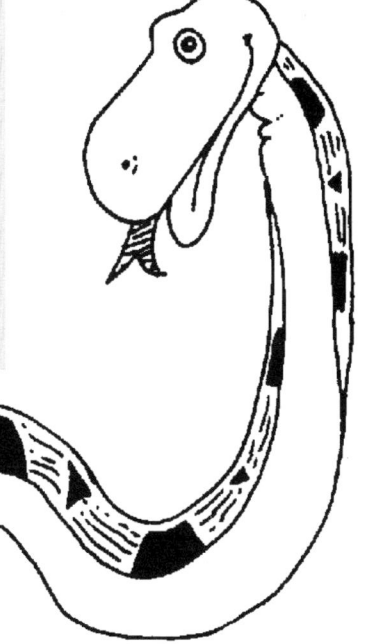

Introduction

The resources in this book are designed to be used with 5 to 7 year olds. In particular, they are intended to support follow-up work on **The Number Crew**, the Channel 4 Schools mathematics series. It is hoped that the photocopiable sheets will help meet the needs of busy teachers who wish to develop interactive whole-class teaching as recommended in the Numeracy Strategy. Some pages are intended to be used by the teacher to provide an interesting focus for a whole-class lesson; others can be used to provide challenging activities as well as guided practice for pupils. Do adapt the sheets to meet the needs of your class — amend or add parts as you wish. Blank versions of some of the sheets have been provided so that you can use the most appropriate numbers, operations and so on for your class.

Contents

Large Digit Cards	5 – 9
Small Number/Symbol Cards	10 – 13
Number Word Cards	14 – 16
Number Grids	17 – 19
Loop Cards	20 – 22
Place Value Cards	23 – 25
Banana Cards	26
Flip-Flaps	27 – 30
Number Crew Characters	31 – 36
Dumbbells	37
Number-Crunching Machine	38
Finger Puppets	39 – 40
Shape Cards	41
Decimetre Sticks	42
Clock Faces	43
Number Crew Time Activities	44

Teacher's Notes

Large Digit Cards (pages 5 – 9)

Washing lines:
Peg the cards onto a washing line to help with oral counting. Extend the line as required. Peg some cards in position as guidelines, give out the rest to members of the class, and ask them in turn, to come and peg them up in the correct positions.

Number tracks:
The numbers can be put on large cards or tiles to make a number track which the children can walk along, saying the numbers as they walk.

Number sentences:
Give large cards to several children to hold up at the front of the class to show two- and three-digit numbers. If you add symbol cards (page 13) number sentences can be made.

'Living' numbers:
Many mathematical games can be played in the hall or playground if each child in the class is given a number to wear. Make number bibs from card and string or more permanent ones from fabric. Younger children can be asked to find someone wearing a number one more or one less than themselves and so on. Older children can be asked to find pairs of numbers which add up to 10, or make sets of odd or even numbers.

Small Number/Symbol Cards (pages 10 – 13)

'Show me' activities:
Give each child a set of cards for a whole-class session. Have the children 'show' a card to answer questions such as: What is the number after 9? Before 20? Between 10 and 15?... You could also put two sets of cards in a bag to pass round the class; children could take out a number and say the number 1 more or 10 more. The children could show you number sentences made using the symbol cards.

Number Word Cards (pages 14 – 16)

These help to clear up confusion about numbers with similar-sounding names. Use them as labels to supplement or replace the large number cards.

Number Grids (pages 17 – 19)

Jigsaws:
Make number 'jigsaws' by photocopying the squares onto card, and cutting into several pieces. Children love putting the pieces together again. More pieces makes the task more difficult. As the children gain confidence, pieces from more than one square can be mixed together.

Laminated squares:
Children can use a washable marker pen to mark off the numbers as they exclude them, in games such as 'spot the number'. The cards can be wiped clean at the end of each game and reused.

Loop Cards (pages 20 – 22)

These can be used to improve skills in mental arithmetic. The 'loop' is composed of six number cards, each of which has a calculation instruction to get to the next number; the last instruction takes the player back to the start and completes the loop.

Children can play individually with one loop, then join others with different loops to play a group game. All the cards are shuffled together and shared between the players. One player starts by putting down a card. The player to the left then follows with the next card. If they do not hold the correct card, they miss a go. Play continues until all the cards are in the loop.

Place Value Cards (pages 23 – 25)

Children can use the cards to represent two- and three-digit numbers by overlaying them in the space marked on the ship (page 25), with the units cards on top. After some experience with the cards, ask them to use just two cards to show numbers like 106 or 409, illustrating the need for zero as a place holder. Whole-class work can be followed by individual or paired work.

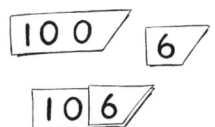

Banana Cards (page 26)

These are 'fun' cards which can be used to measure things. Made into a 'bunch' of bananas, the cards can be used during a 'show me' session, in place of 0 – 9 number cards.

Flip-Flaps (pages 27 – 30)

These are very useful for work on number bonds, particularly when children are trying to learn facts by heart. Enlarge the flip-flaps to make demonstration models. To make them last longer, photocopy them onto thin card.

Flip-flap 1 (page 27):
Once the class have agreed that there are 10 animals, ask the children to fold down one animal and ask how many they can see. When they reply 'nine', you can give them the fact that nine and one make ten. Do similar activities until you have covered all the number bonds to 10.

Flip-flap 2 (page 28):
This flip-flap is good for teaching addition and subtraction facts to 5. When the children are confident with the addition facts (4 + 1, 3 + 2, and so on), point out that if they know these facts then they also know that 5 – 1 = 4 and 5 – 3 = 2, and so on. Ask them to write number sentences as they fold down the animals.

Flip-flap 3 (page 29):
This arrangement of squares can be used for an assessment activity. Children who are not certain of the number facts to 10 can be encouraged to work with a partner. One child folds the flip-flap to show different numbers of animals; the other child has to say how many more animals would make 10.

Flip-flap 4 (page 30):
This has been left blank so that children can make a flip-flap using their own drawings or the characters on page 31.

Number Crew Characters (pages 31 – 36)

Use the outlines of the characters and the boat to prepare other activities in the classroom. Encouraging children to talk and write about what they have learned is a way of consolidating their learning as well as an opportunity to find out what they are thinking. This is important when the aim is to encourage children to work things out mentally whenever they can.

Dumbbells (page 37)

Enter a number into the central square. Ask the children to take turns to select two numbers which together add up to that number. Use with individuals as an assessment activity.

Number-Crunching Machine (page 38)

This is useful for practice using the four operations on different sets of numbers. The operation, as well as the input numbers, can be changed according to the children's abilities.

Finger Puppets (pages 39 – 40)

Helping the children to make these puppets provides an opportunity for the use of mathematical language, as well as practice with number bonds. Encourage the children to invent number stories using the puppets.

Shape Cards (page 41)

Children can play 'snap' games with several sets of cards. Talking about the shapes helps children to recognise the essential attributes of shapes.

Decimetre Sticks (page 42)

These are useful when children are measuring length. Putting measures end to end is much easier that moving one measure along.

Clock Faces and Number Crew Time Activities (pages 43 – 44)

Appropriate matching activities can be devised using the clock faces and the pictures of activities.

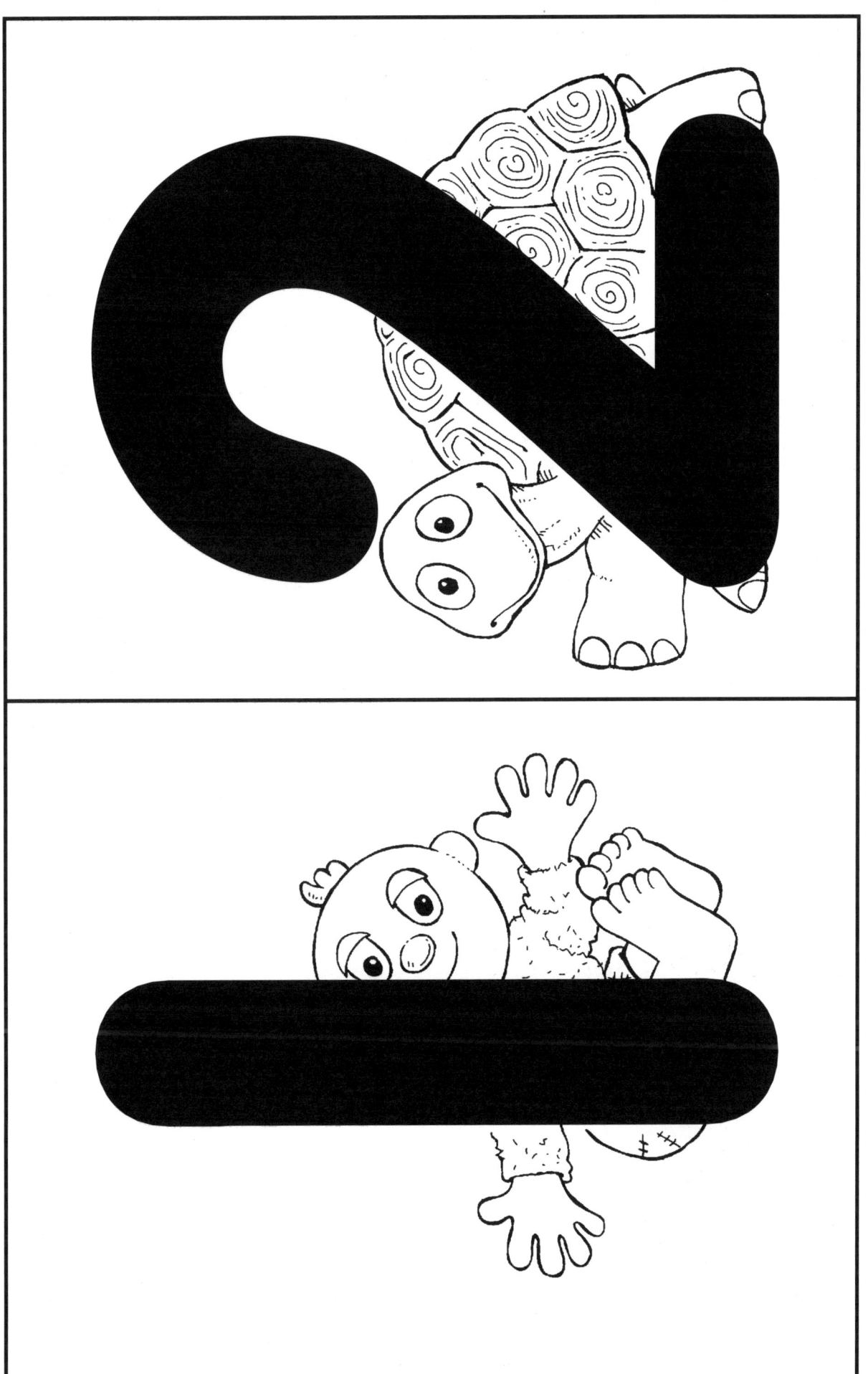

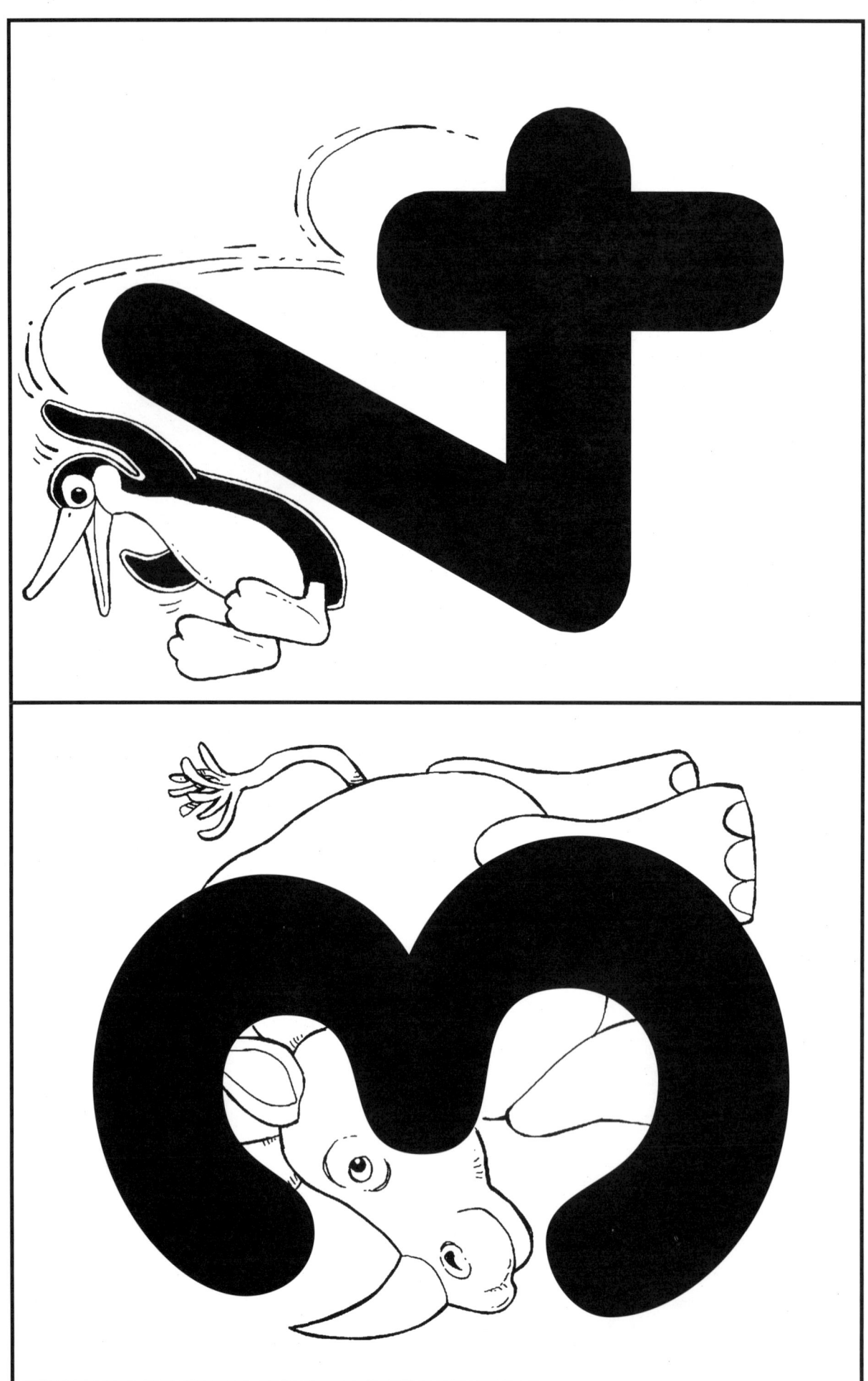

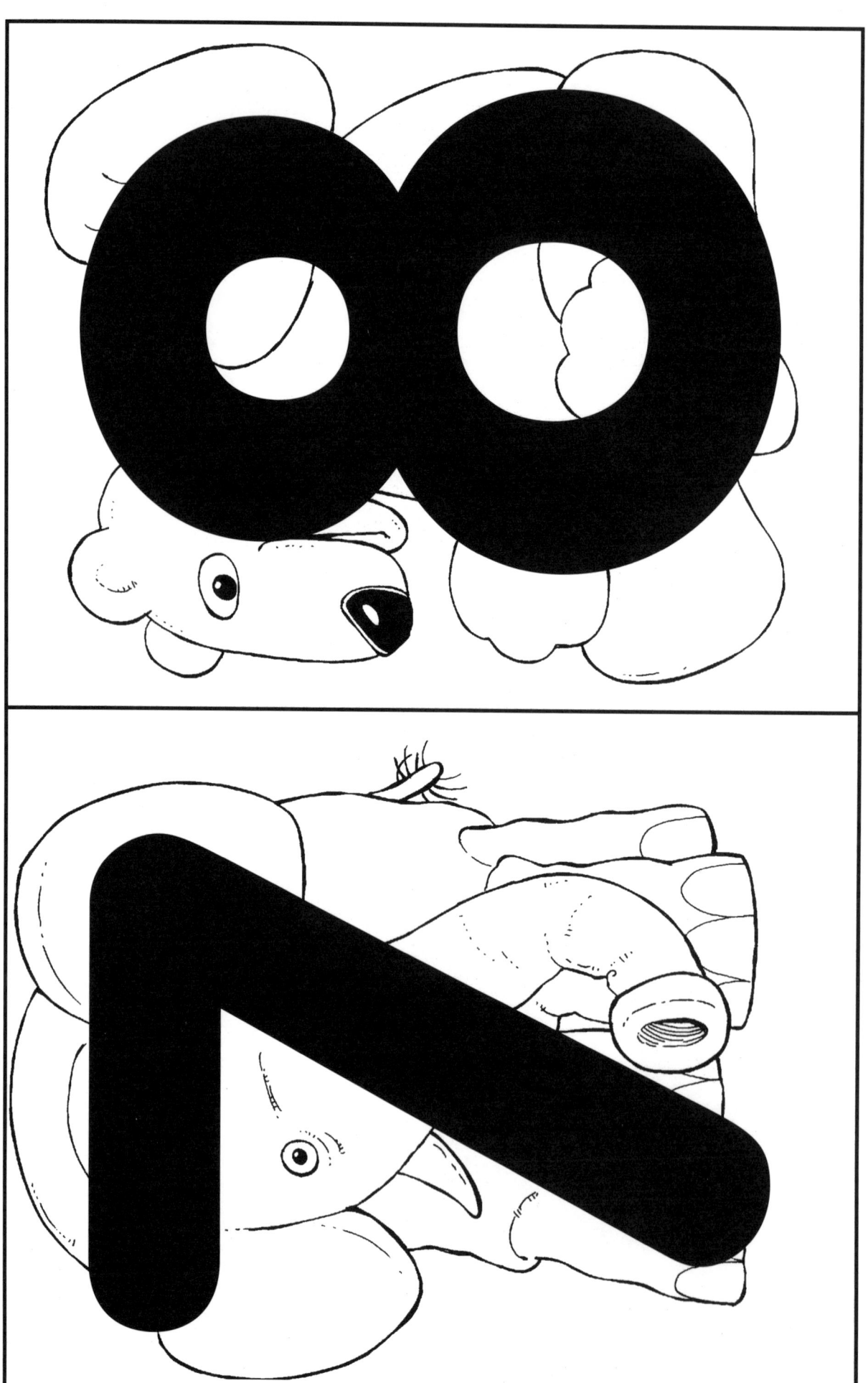

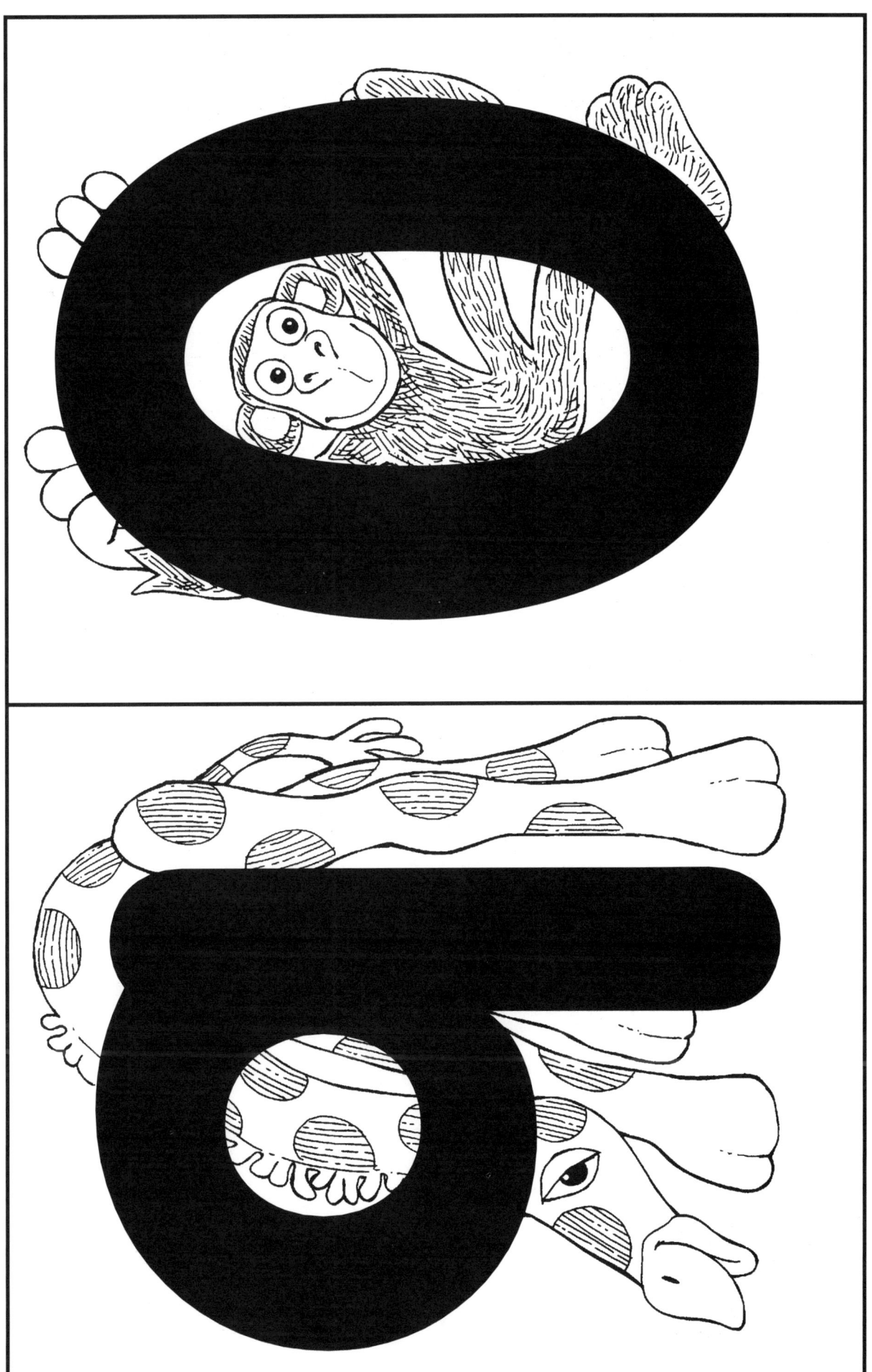

The Number Crew © 1999 Channel Four Learning

Small Number/Symbol Cards

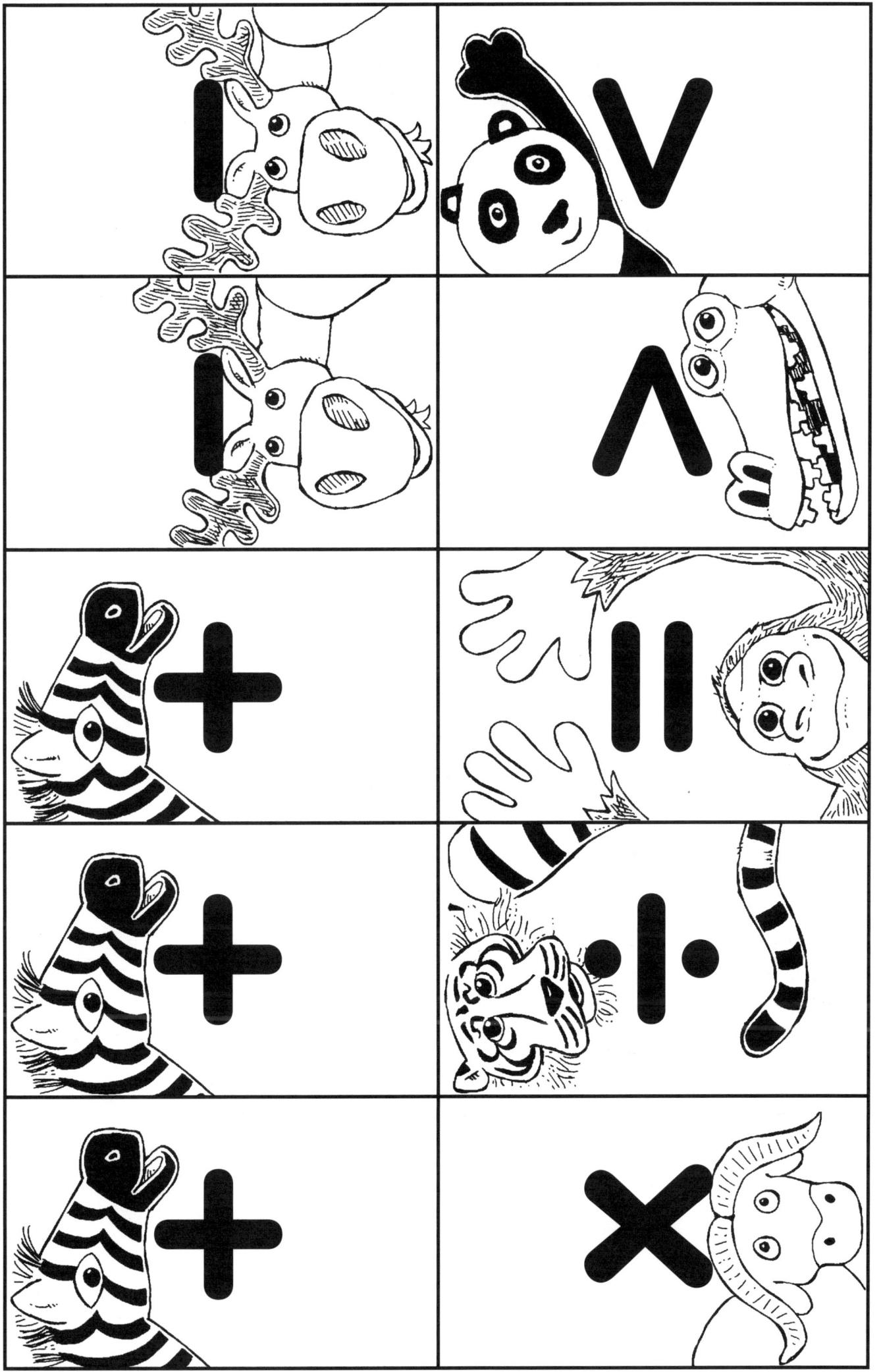

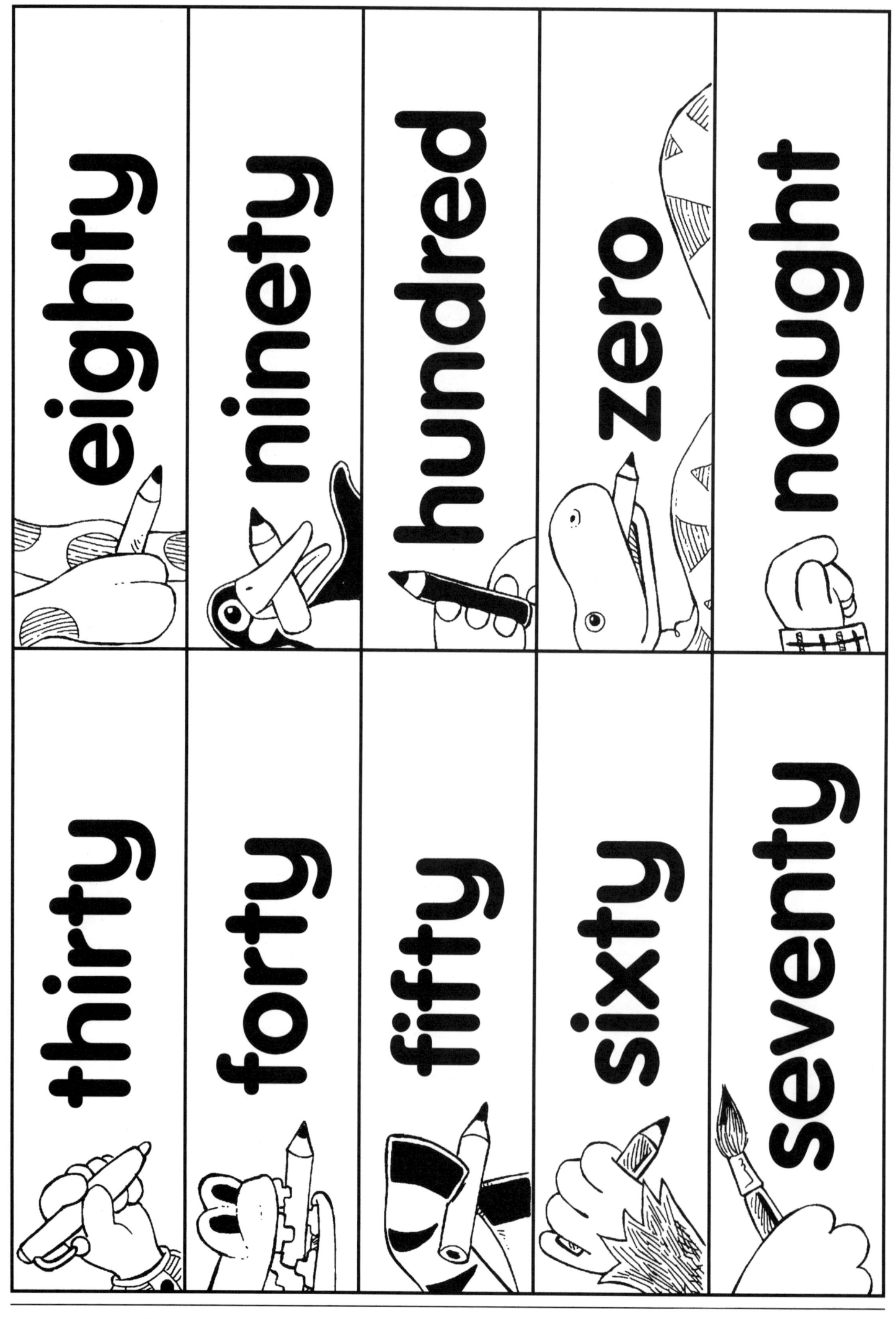

1	2	3	4	5	6	7	8	9	10
11	12	13	14	15	16	17	18	19	20
21	22	23	24	25	26	27	28	29	30
31	32	33	34	35	36	37	38	39	40
41	42	43	44	45	46	47	48	49	50
51	52	53	54	55	56	57	58	59	60
61	62	63	64	65	66	67	68	69	70
71	72	73	74	75	76	77	78	79	80
81	82	83	84	85	86	87	88	89	90
91	92	93	94	95	96	97	98	99	100

The Number Crew © 1999 Channel Four Learning

Number Grids

0	1	2	3	4	5	6	7	8	9
10	11	12	13	14	15	16	17	18	19
20	21	22	23	24	25	26	27	28	29
30	31	32	33	34	35	36	37	38	39
40	41	42	43	44	45	46	47	48	49
50	51	52	53	54	55	56	57	58	59
60	61	62	63	64	65	66	67	68	69
70	71	72	73	74	75	76	77	78	79
80	81	82	83	84	85	86	87	88	89
90	91	92	93	94	95	96	97	98	99

The Number Crew © 1999 Channel Four Learning

Number Grids

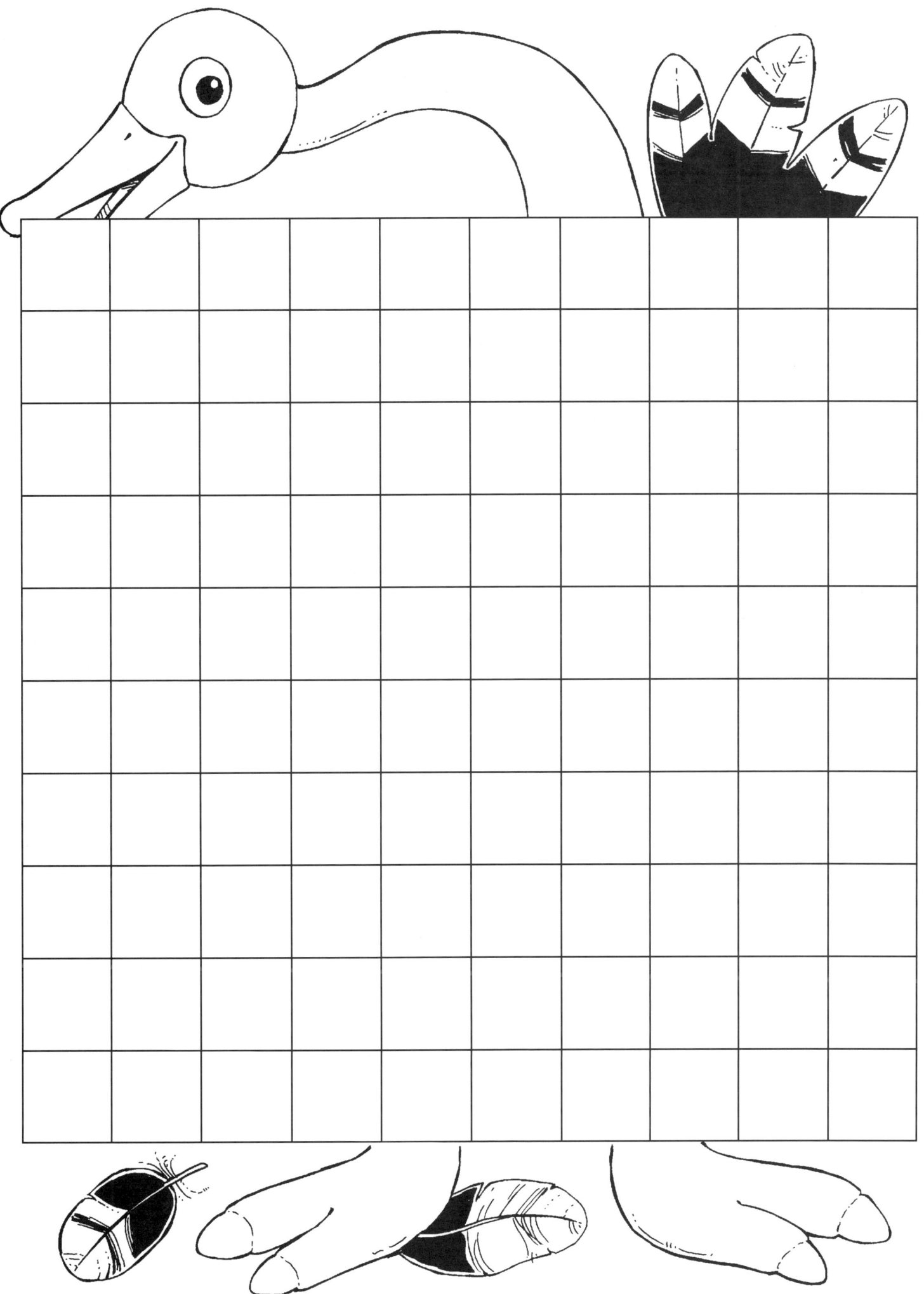

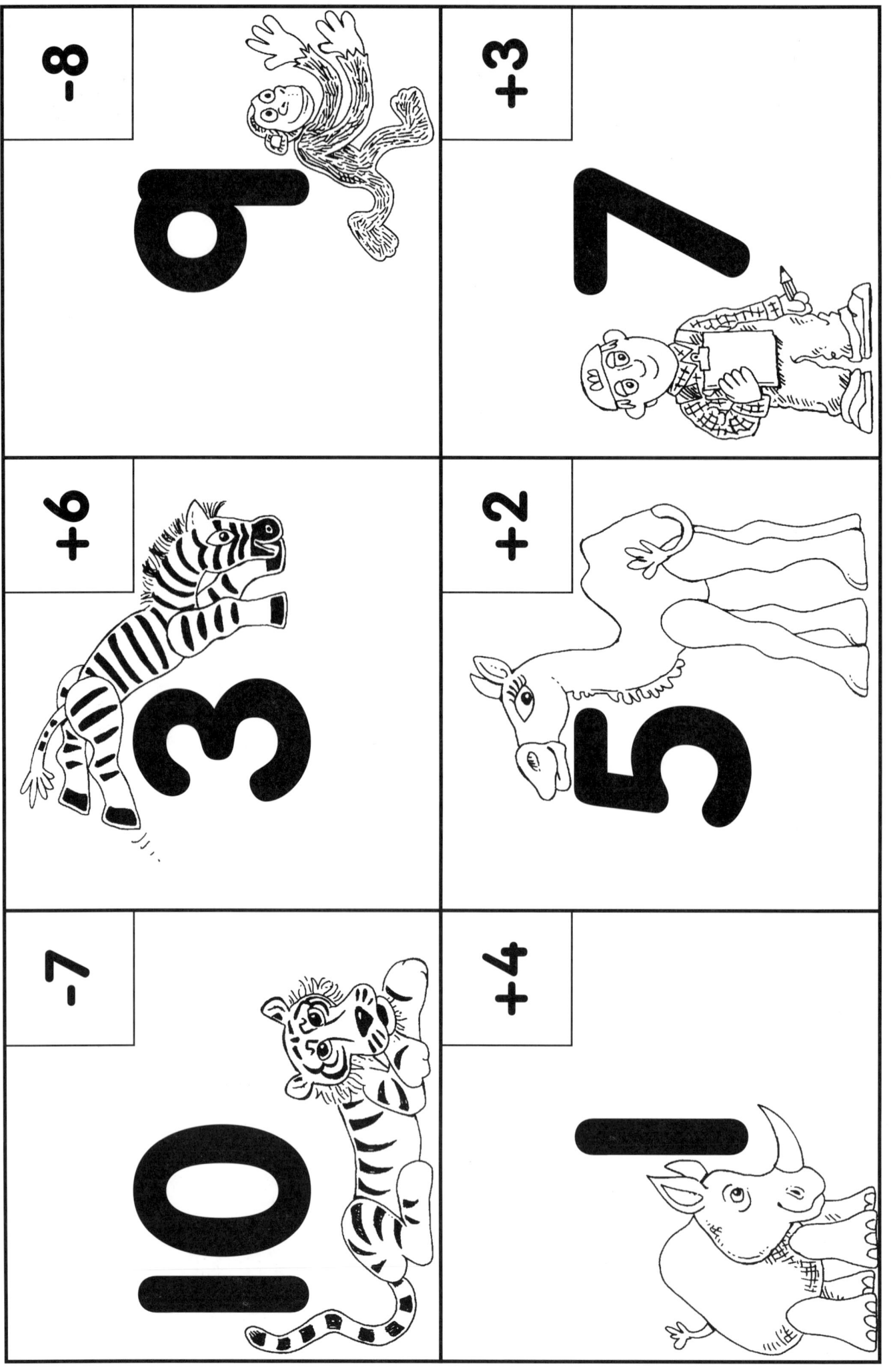

9 0 0	9
8 0 0	8
	9 0
8 0	7 0
6 0	5 0
4 0	3 0
2 0	1 0

The Number Crew © 1999 Channel Four Learning — Place Value Cards

1	100
2	200
3	300
4	400
5	500
6	600
7	700

The Number Crew © 1999 Channel Four Learning — Place Value Cards

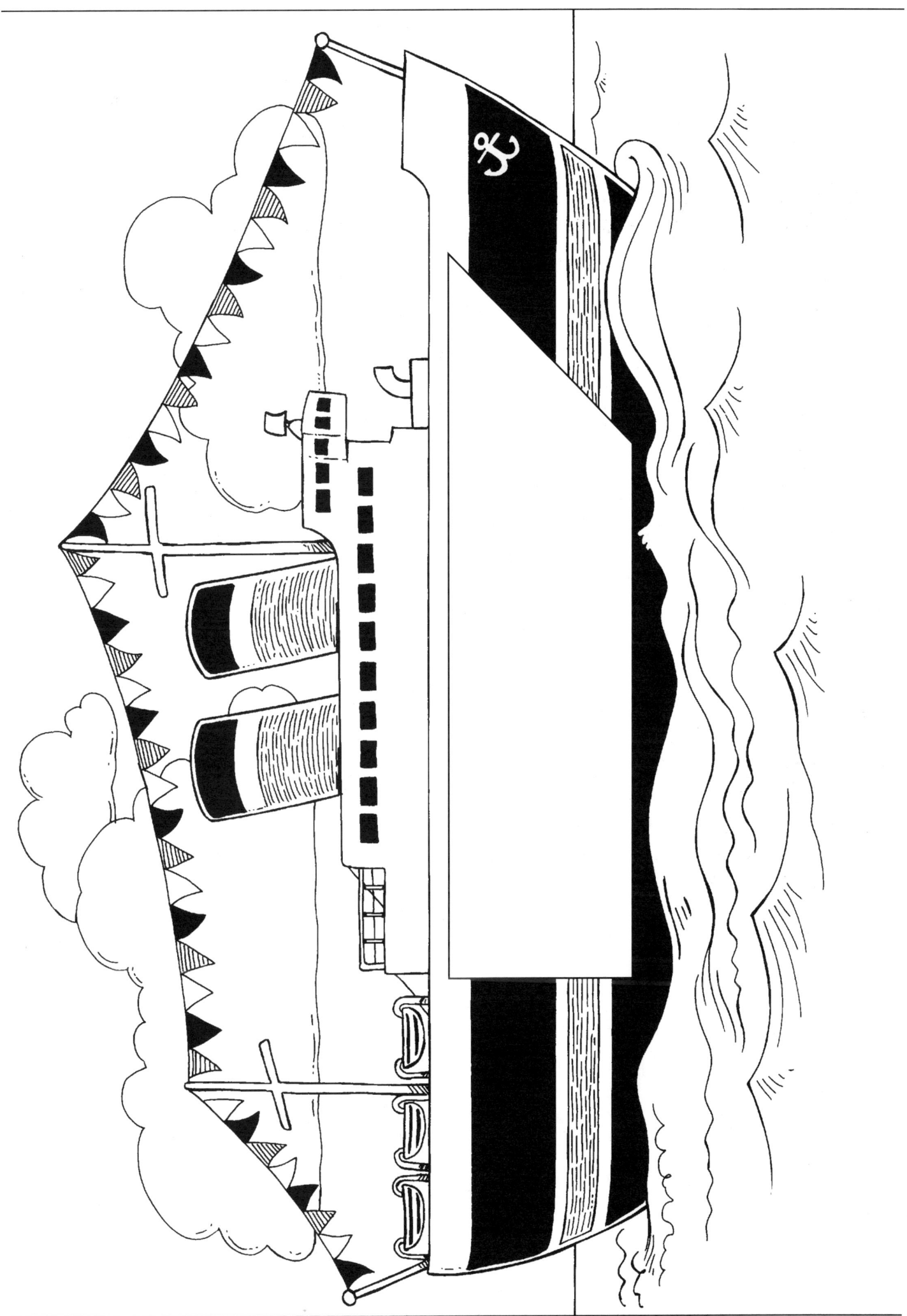

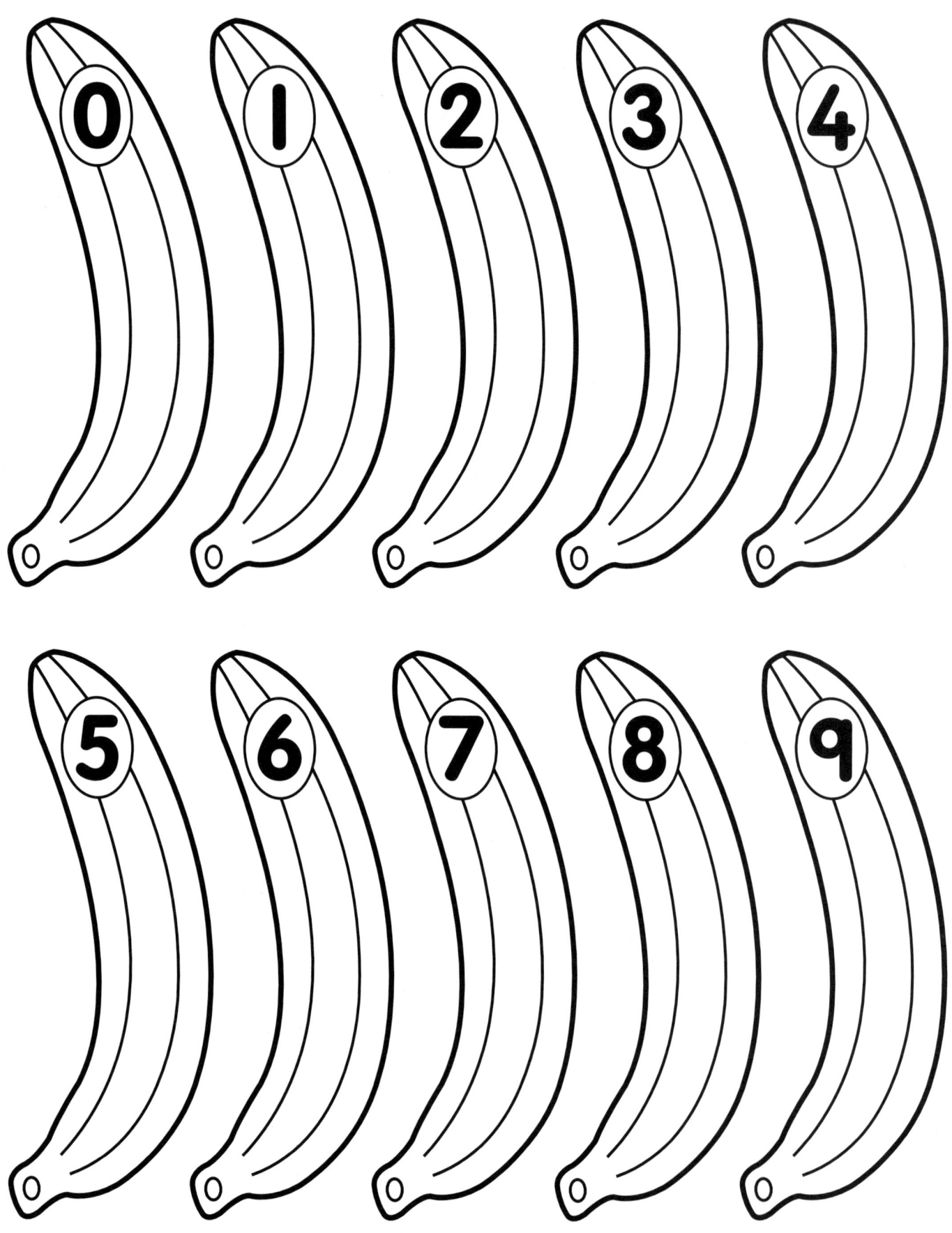

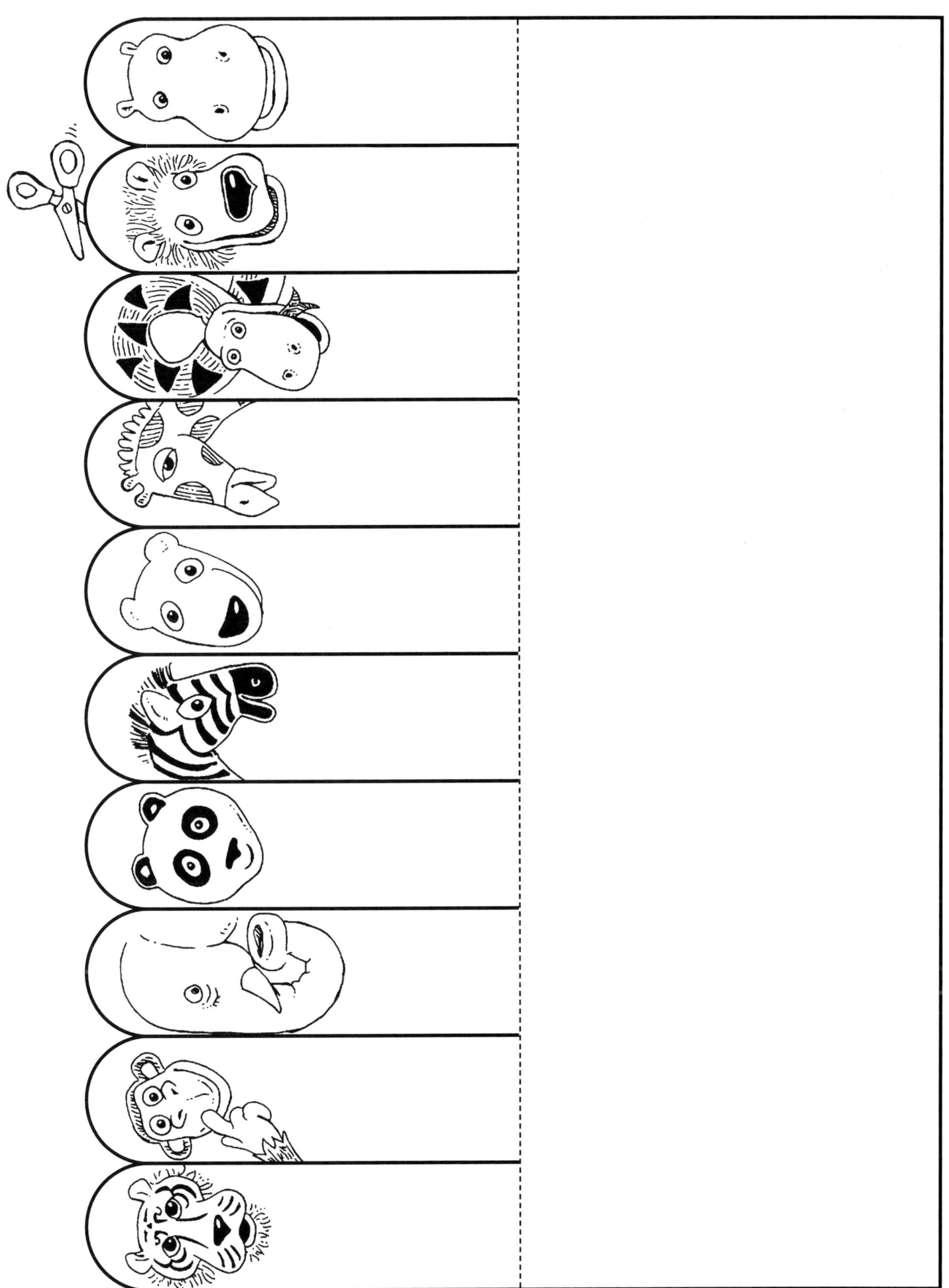

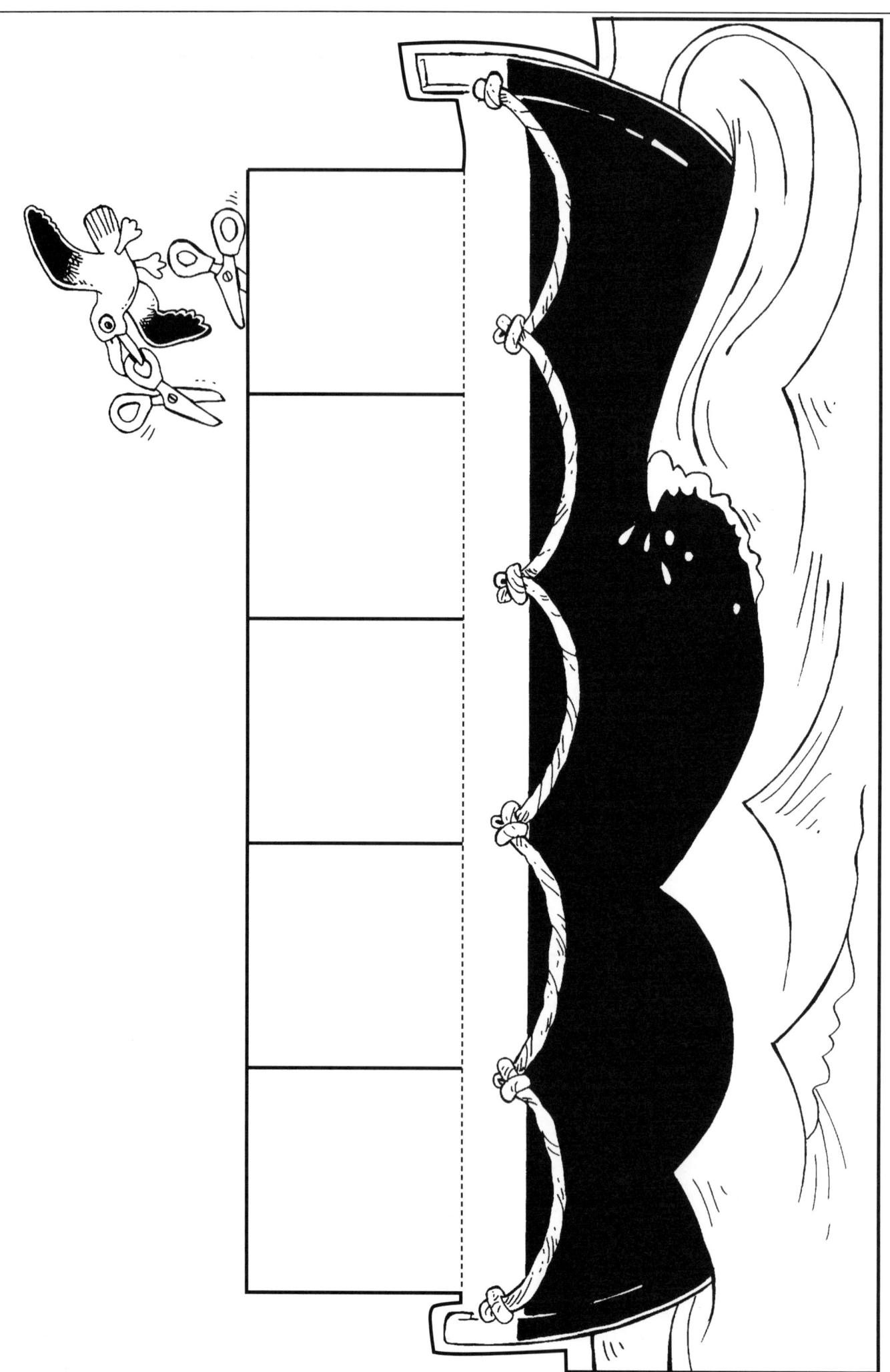

The Number Crew © 1999 Channel Four Learning

Number Crew Characters

The Number Crew © 1999 Channel Four Learning

Number Crew Characters

Ted	Fiz
Mirabelle	Bradley
Flo	Baby Bunting
lion	snake
moose	rhino
panda	polar bear
gorilla	elephant
camel	zebra
hippo	kangaroo
penguin	buffalo
giraffe	ostrich
tiger	crocodile
monkey	turtle

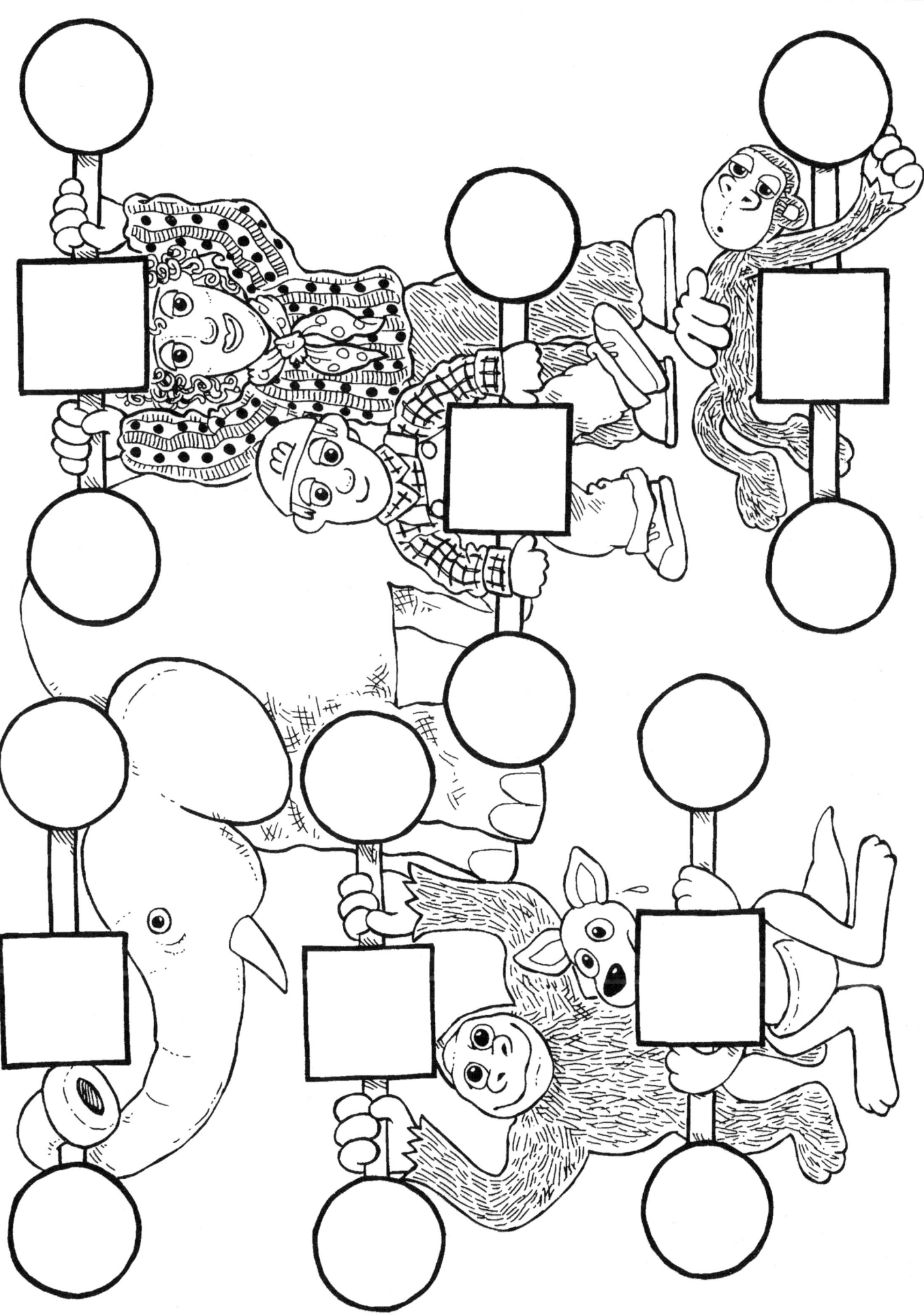

Number-Crunching Machine

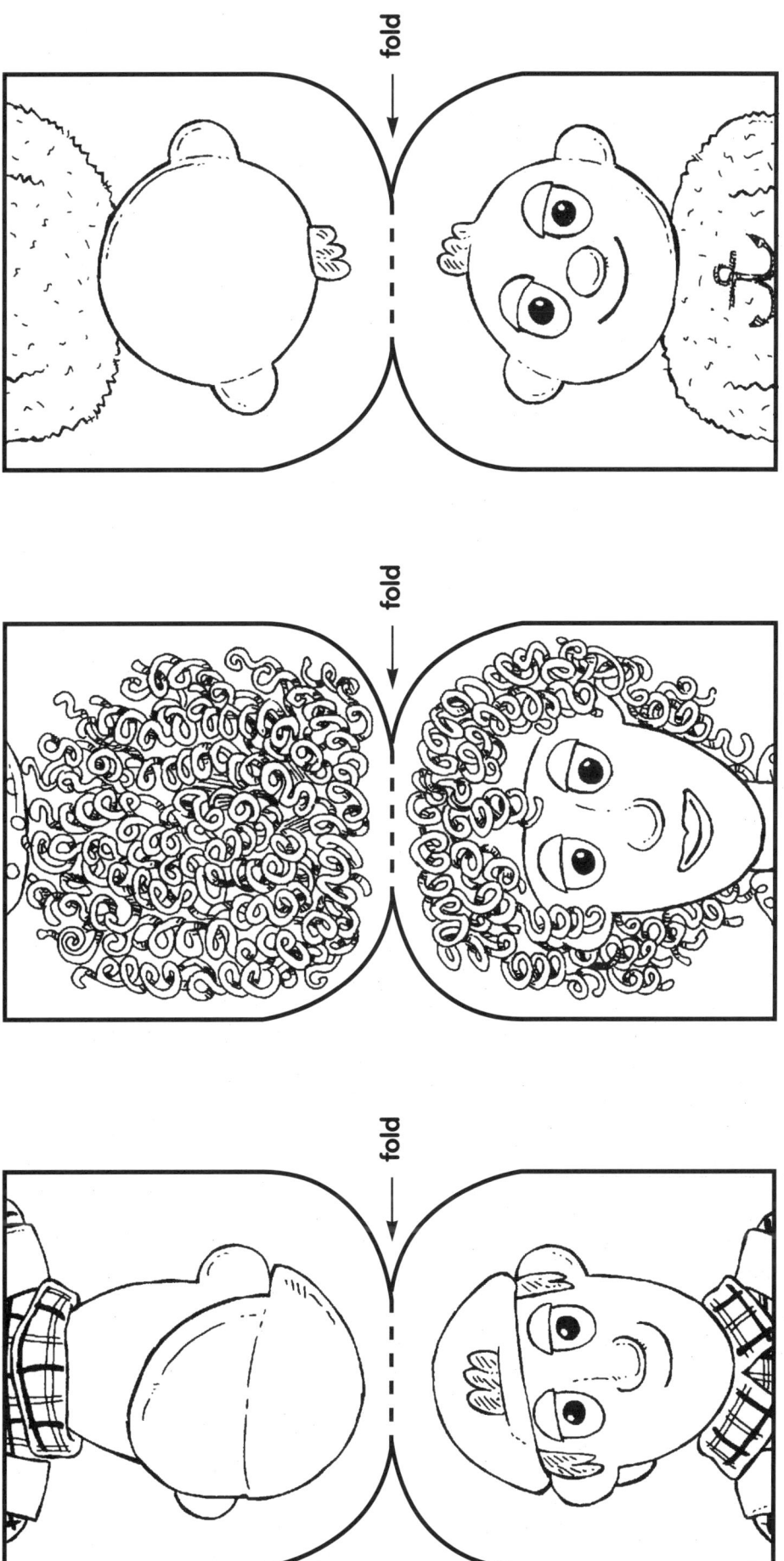

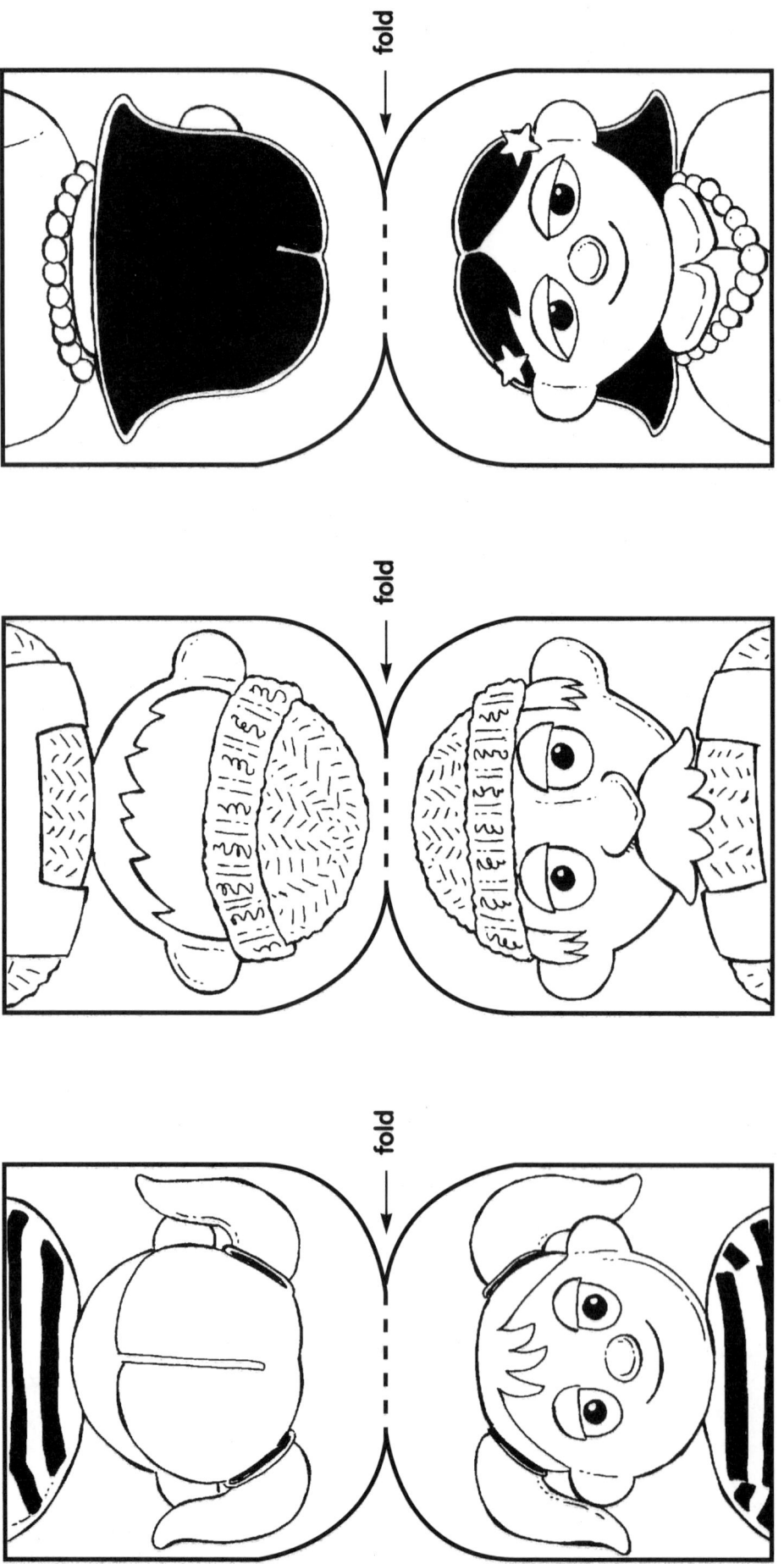

The Number Crew © 1999 Channel Four Learning   Finger Puppets

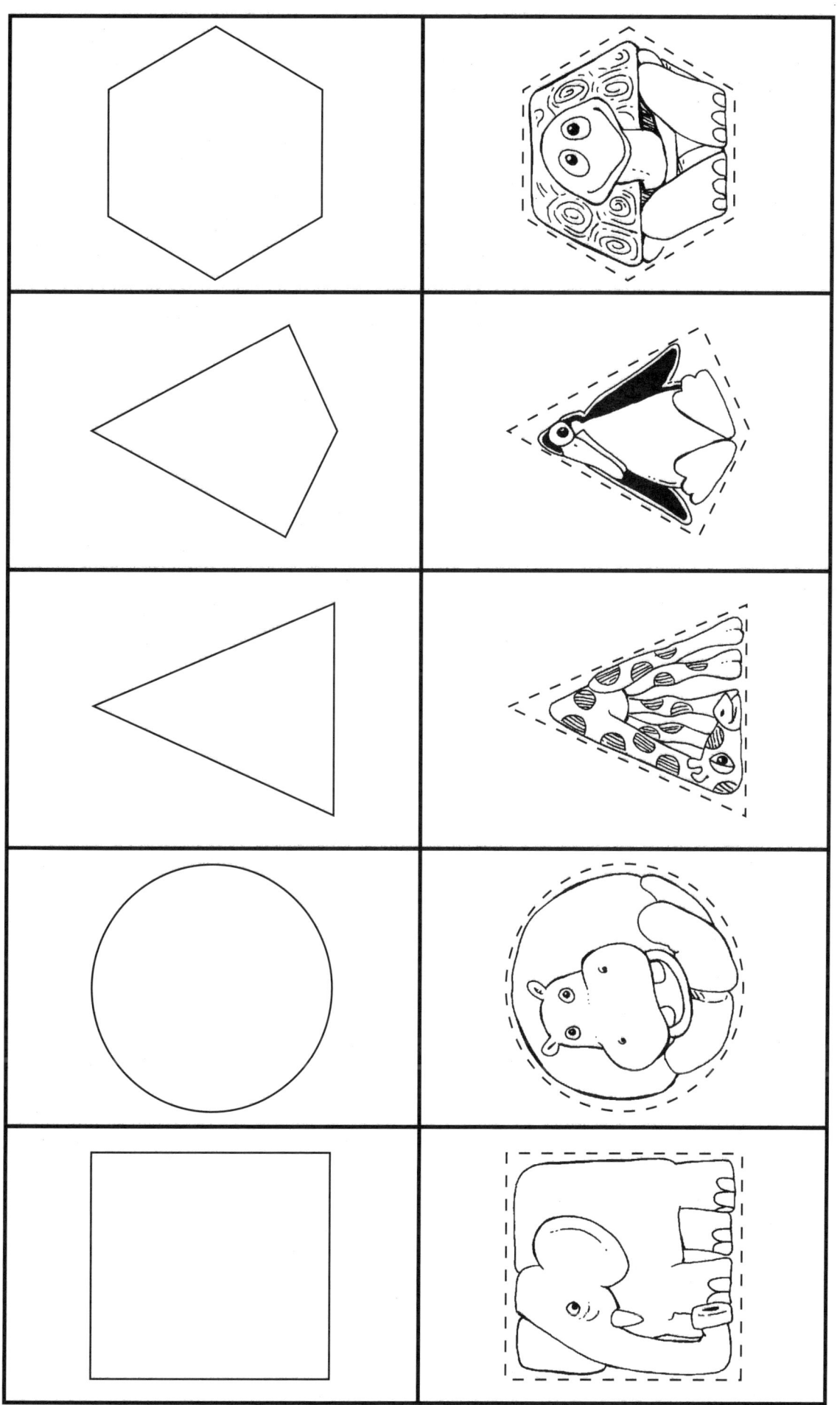

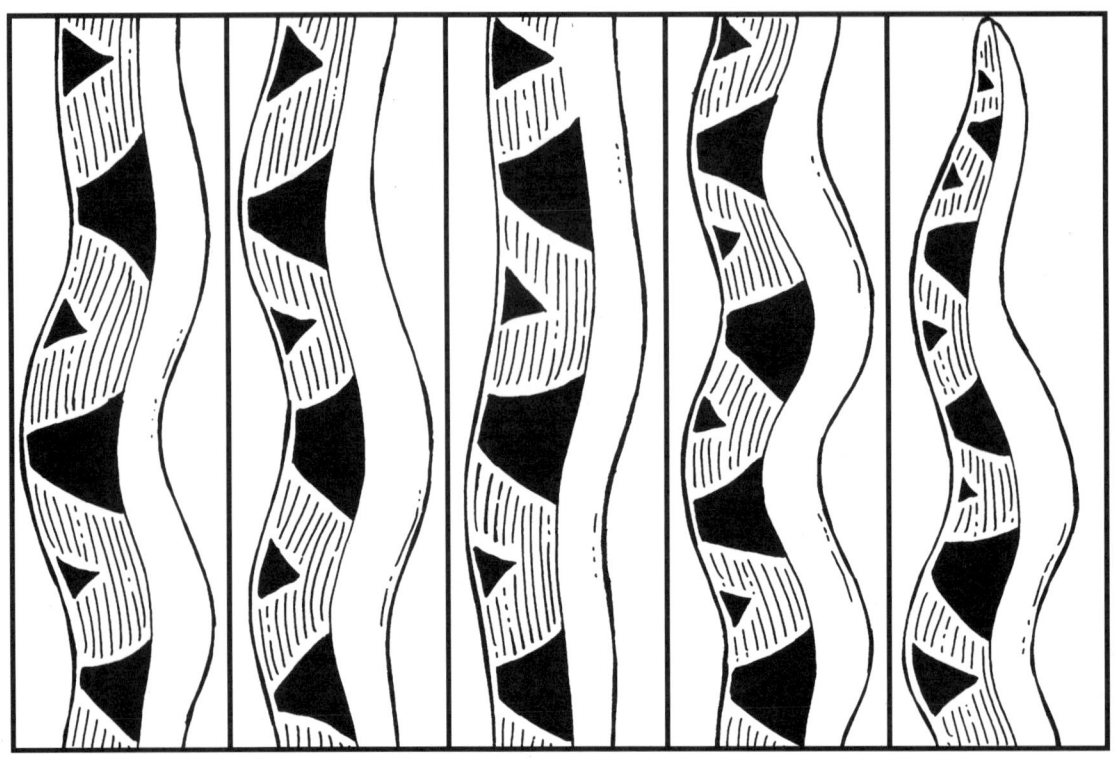
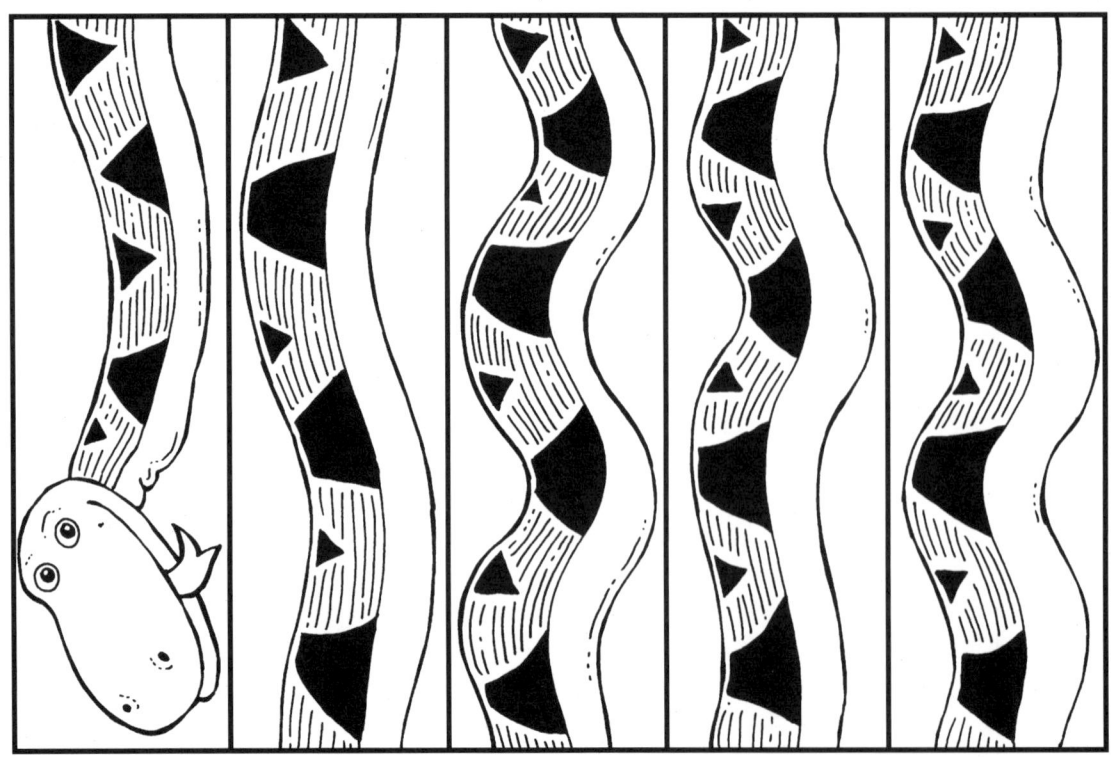

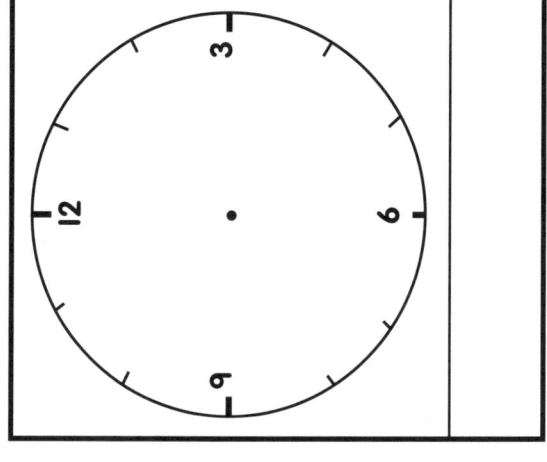
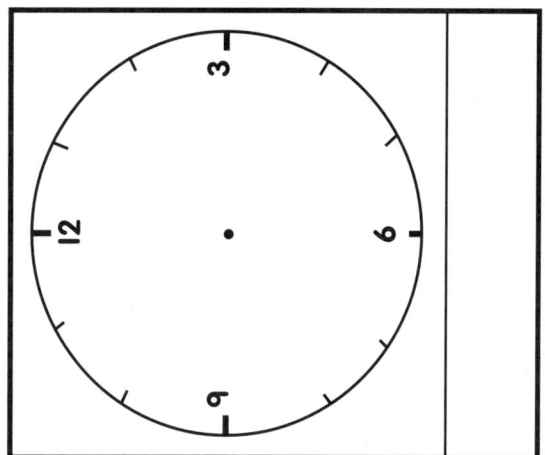
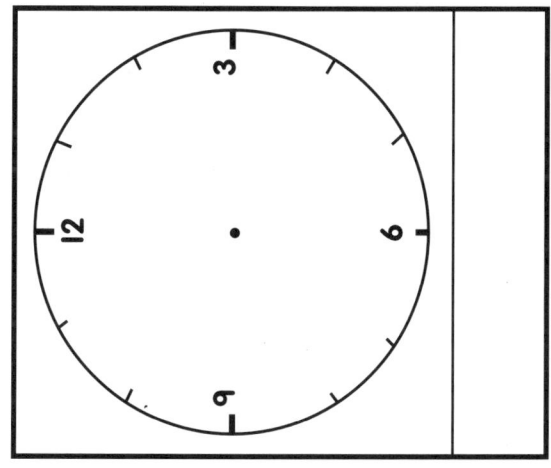
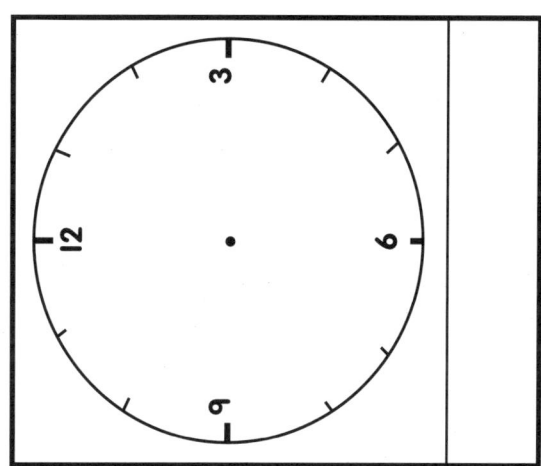
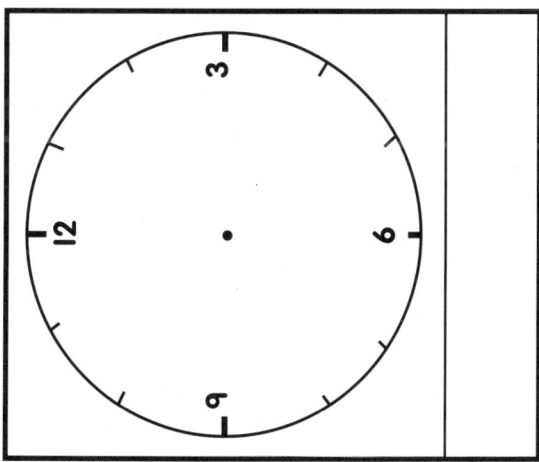
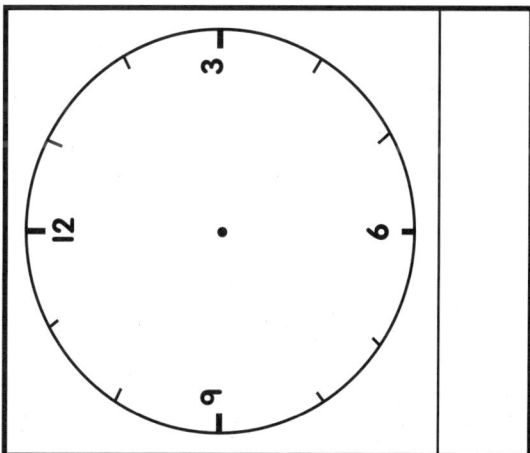

The Number Crew © 1999 Channel Four Learning — Clock Faces